Heal

Healing the Darkness

Melissa Barnes

VANTAGE PRESS
New York

Cover design by Susan Thomas

FIRST EDITION

Published by Vantage Press, Inc.
419 Park Ave. South, New York, NY 10016

Manufactured in the United States of America
ISBN: 0-533-14466-3

Library of Congress Catalog Card No.: 2002095212

0 9 8 7 6 5 4 3 2 1

Contents

Healing the Darkness

The Key

Searching for the key
It's inside of me
What can be will be.

Open wide my soul door
Out my love will pour
Never again to be sore.

This is my gate
There is no hate
I am the mate.

Regaining my wondrous dreams
Playing in ethereal streams
Silencing the screams.

Child

Child
     so sweet
     so kind
I'm so glad you're mine.

Child
     so young
     so blind
I really don't mind.

Child
     so beautiful
     so bright
I'll hold you tight.

Child
     so bold
     so daring
I won't stop caring.

Child
     so cute
     still talking
Let's start walking.

The Gate

Love is a guise
To the material guys.

Hate is their mate
So close the gate.

Locked away from sight
They curse their blight.

Hate spawns hate
Lock tight the gate.

My Rhyme

This is just for me.
A special little rhyme
To mark this place in time.

Lost in line,
No space or time,
Memories unfold
So grab ahold.

Just a little longer,
You'll grow stronger.
Expanding the space,
Quickening the pace.

Holding your face,
Picturing the place.
Fighting the Pain,
My memories retain.

Losing my place,
Slowing the pace,
Sliding through space,
Banishing your face.

Memories untold,
Cannot unfold.
No power or pain
Will remain.

Serenity and peace
Are the feast.

Poor Woman

Complaints fall free
People torture me
Just let me be.

What belief
Common thief
No relief.

Blood-hungry leech
Dead people preach
Fix the breach.

Creature within
Person is dim
Her chances slim.

People

Toltarian Time
Question and rhyme
Human slime.

Aquarian age
Dial and page
Life's stage.

Scorpions' sting
Bracelet and ring
Stolen thing.

Sagittarian advice
Pasta and rice
People are lice.

Buddy

I'm wild and free
Let my soul be
Run away with me.

Soft, cute and furry
Always in a hurry
Let my memories stay unblurry.

Stretch, yawn and crawl
I've grown up tall
Remember when I was small?

Holding me as I die
Now please don't cry
I wish I could say good-bye.

All I can do is shudder and sigh.

I LOVE YOU, BUDDY.

Greed

Memories sold
All for gold.

Greed for You
Is too true.

Memories saved
All I craved.

Pain for me
Will always be.

Work

Life is so fleeting,
Fragile at best.
We work all day long,
Just so we can rest!

Up at first light,
WORK, WORK, WORK.
This can't be right,
Working till night!

We come home late,
But please don't despair!
Watch the news at eight,
Fall asleep in our chair.

Tomorrow's a new day,
So WORK, WORK, WORK!
But make time to play,
That's life's only quirk.

Attunement

Shining Sun
Shooting Stars
Smoking Gun.

Ghostly Moon
Dancing Shadows
Haunting Tune.

Mourning Trees
Whispering Winds
Silent Pleas.

Chaos

Roaring Waves
Thunderous Rains
Conditions Unchanged.

Turbulent Tides
Untouched Skies
Emotional Cries.

Torrential Floods
Acid Rain
Uncontrollable Pain.

Raging Winds
Wild Fires
Unholy Sires.

Situations

Scars inside
Darkness hides
Imperfect brides.

Excuses galore
Old folk lore
Want some more.

So dark and dreary
I'm so weary
Don't get teary.

Horrible demise
Simple compromise
You despise.

Blue

NO distance too far
Love as you are.

NO story untold
Please be bold.

NO soft summer sigh
Just a warm good-bye.

NO memories of pain
I love in vain.

NO thoughts of you
Now I am blue.

Silent Crescendo

Roaring silence
A quiet shout
The brightest oblivion
Features a pout.

Crescendos unheard
The unspoken word
No musical melody
The feeling's absurd.

Alone in the silence
Deafening to my ears
My hell is muteness
My life is tears.

Featureless faces
Crowd in my mind
No beautiful portrait
For me to find.

Quest

A lifetime of pain
For one summer's gain
There is NO shame.

Life's only been true
To feeling blue
I'll fight through.

Experience is the quest
So do your best
You are just a guest.

Time's running short
Please be a sport
Bring your ship to port.

Hearts of Gold

Moonlit skies
Warm good-byes

Treasured times
Heart of mine

Feelings unspoken
Hearts unbroken

Desires fulfilled
Definitely thrilled

Vibrantly alive
Our love thrives.

Psyche

Seeing with mystical eyes
Hearing each and all cries
Searching the midnight skies.

Cleansing my mind
Seeking my kind
Feeling I'm blind.

Seeing further in time
Completely lost in this line
Never seeing behind.

Reaching toward the star
Never moving far
It's left a scar.

Just Dreams

Land of streams
Bloodless Screams
Spiritual are the dreams.

Pure energy form
Minus emotional storms
Beings beyond the norm.

Freedom from the senses
Loss of menses
Life outside fences.

Knowledge is recalled
Energy beings appalled
Research is stalled.

Recognition is bad
Humans become sad
Energy forms are cads.

Steer clear of swirling lights
Humans pray during nights
Energy forms carry blights.

Your Kind

I'm not that blind
I know your kind
Please stay behind.

We're lost in debate
I feel your hate
I'm not your mate.

One foot out the door
My tears simply pour
Destroyed at the core.

You never listen to me
Why can't you see?
This isn't meant to be.

Finally at long last
I'm clear of the blast
Will I learn from the past?

Our Hearts

How can you be
So unkind to me?

So hard is your heart
When will you start?

Understanding the tones
Of the love you have thrown.

Complete or in part
Will you love with your heart?

Beating ever so slow
Can you withstand the blow?

Whatever you hold dear
My heart holds near.

For in my own heart
I love you, not in part.

I shall wait and see
Whatever you will be.

Evolution

Dedicated devotion
　　Unrivaled emotion.

Twisted existence
　　Daily persistence.

Heated debate
　　Unforgiving mate.

Unbelievable lies
　　Grief-filled sighs.

Hopeless tries
　　Tortured cries.

Sanity flees
　　Crazy pleas.

Awful illusions
　　Simple conclusions.

Death and Destruction
　　Spiritual construction.

Mom

You soothed away my pain,
Walked with me in the rain.

Loved me each and every day,
Even when I pushed you away.

You helped me to stand,
When I would have ran.

Listened to all my complaints,
With love, wisdom, and restraint.

You've helped me to understand,
Just how I fit into the plan.

Thank you for the lift,
Your love is such a precious gift.

Mountain World

Look at the mountains
so lovely to behold.

Sitting so majestically,
in a royal purple robe.

With flowers as a carpet
and blue skies as a roof.

The trees are our shelter,
The animals our hosts.

You

Out of the blue,
     I found you.

Into the dark,
     You plunged my heart.

Miraculously saved,
     By a heart so brave.

I heard your song,
     You cared all along.

The Transition

Death is only a door
Light and warmth at our core
I feel my soul smoor[*]
Love and acceptance galore.

Life is only a dream
Tearing apart at the seam
So please don't scream
Feel the sun beam.

The real world awaits
Throw open the gates
Let go of the hate
Hurry now, don't be late.

*Smoor is a Scottish Gaelic term for covering the fire at night.

Fading Away

I'm seeking solace and control.
Work has taken its toll.
The quiet seeps into my soul.

I'm not a contender.
My body has rendered.
I will peacefully surrender.

I've been left with little doubt.
My body's tired from this last bout.
I feel a gentle warmth from without.

I'm tired of using my fists.
I've lost all my useless empty lists.
I'm fading away into the mists.

Fearless

Fearless you say
Courage during day
Darkness at bay
Lost in dismay.

Pouring spring rain
One original stain
Feeling your pain
I'm not insane.

Searing summer heat
We're dancing dead meat
Painless stupid feat
White as a sheet.

Endless stormy skies
Blood-stained cries
Forever final good-byes
Everyone fades and dies.

Over Time

Emptiness reigns
Silent tune
Growth pains.

Everlasting light
Darkest moon
Psychic fight.

Unconditional love
Silver spoon
Spiritual shove.

Beautiful life
Graceful loon
Devastating strife.

Rolling ocean
Playful raccoon
Restricted motion.

Moonlit nights
Summer's noon
Surprising delights.

Old-growth pine
Animals boon
Racing time.

My Love

Caught in the rain,
I still feel the pain.

Memories of you
Come crashing through.

It's all I can do
to stay away from you.

When will I learn,
I can never return?

The love we once shared
Is beyond all repair.

The Greatest Accomplishment

The greatest accomplishment
I've yet to see
Is the love of a man
And him of me
No lies to be told
No stories unfold
Dropping the facade
No macho tirades
Losing the shame
Ending the game.

In winning the game
You've created shame
The illusion of love
Will give to shove
Before it's too late
Reconsider my fate.

Natural Order

Molten liquid mountains
Wandering ghostly plains
Dead desert stains

Ethereal motion
Whiplash gales
Misty trails

Rolling water
Thunderous waves
Flying sprays

Burning obsession
Living flames
Wildfire tames

Searing Breeze
Zephyrs sneeze
Cirrus clouds tease

Cosmos

Blossom on the vine
Deadly heart of mine
Show me a sign

Crossing stars collide
Passion starts to slide
Comets to ride

Golden people arrive
Elders might survive
Cosmic overdrive

Blue planet stew
Cosmic people view
Earth bound brew

Silent outcries
Bloody good-byes
Shattering sighs

Super heated debate
Dead people late
Loving emotional hate

Quiet killer screams
Lethal cure creams
Waking night dreams